FREEDOM of RELIGION

STEPHANIE HOOVER

Gareth Stevens
PUBLISHING

Please visit our website, www.garethstevens.com.
For a free color catalog of all our high-quality books,
call toll free 1-800-542-2595 or fax 1-877-542-2596.

Cataloging-in-Publication Data

Names: Hoover, Stephanie.
Title: Freedom of religion / Stephanie Hoover.
Description: New York : Gareth Stevens Publishing, 2017. | Series: Our basic freedoms | Includes index.
Identifiers: ISBN 9781482461060 (pbk.) | ISBN 9781482461848 (library bound) | ISBN 9781482461077 (6 pack)
Subjects: LCSH: Freedom of religion--United States--Juvenile literature. | Religion and state--United
States--Juvenile literature.
Classification: LCC BR516.H66 2017 | DDC 323.44'20973--dc23

Published in 2017 by
Gareth Stevens Publishing
111 East 14th Street, Suite 349
New York, NY 10003

Developed and Produced by Focus Strategic Communications, Inc.
Project Manager: Adrianna Edwards
Editor: Ron Edwards
Layout and Composition: Laura Brady, Ruth Dwight
Copyeditors: Adrianna Edwards, Francine Geraci
Media Researchers: Maria DeCambra, Adrianna Edwards
Proofreader: Francine Geraci
Index: Ron Edwards

Photo Credits: Credit Abbreviations: LOC Library of Congress; NARA National Archives and Records Administration; S Shutterstock; WC Wikimedia Commons. Position on the page: T: top, C: center, B: bottom, L: left,
R: right. Zurijeta/S; ; 4: White House Collection/White House Historical Association; 5: Everett Historical/S;
6: Everett Historical/S; 7: Everett Historical/S; 8: Vkilikov/S; 9: Everett Historical/S; 10: Everett Historical/S;
11: Richard Cavalleri/S; 12: Les byerley/S; 13: Everett Historical/S; 14: Jeff Kern/WC; 15: Henryk Sadura/S; 16:
Val Thoermer/S; 17: Anelina/S; 18: Loraks/S; 19: Rsooll/S; 20: LOC/LC-USZ62-110237; 21: Maksim/WC; 23:
Alexander Image/S; 24: BrAt82/S; 25: PixelDarkroom/S; 26: John Foxe/WC; 27: Juan Camilo Bernal/S; 28: John
F. Kennedy Presidential Library and Museum/AR7969-E; 29: GreetingsEarthling/WC; 30: Billion Photos/S;
31: vainillaychile/S; 32: R. MACKAY PHOTOGRAPHY, LLC/S; 33: LOC/LC-DIG-pga-05259; 34: LOC/LC-
USZ62-14693; 35: Travis Puderbaugh/WC; 36: LOC/LC-USF34-036592-D; 37: Christin Lola/S; 38: Lightspring/S;
39: Joseph Sohm/S; 40: Delphi234/WC; 41: Legacy Images/S; 42: Ducu59us/S; 44: Everett - Art/S; 45 T: Everett
Historical/S; 45 B: Rawpixel.com/S.

Printed in the United States of America

CPSIA compliance information: Batch CW17GS: For further information contact
Gareth Stevens, New York, New York at 1-800-542-2595.

CONTENTS

CHAPTER 1

THE ORIGIN OF THE BILL OF RIGHTS

COMPROMISE NEEDED

Like the parties of today, political parties during the 1790s disagreed on many issues. After the United States Constitution was adopted, one party—the Anti-Federalists—worried it gave the federal government far too much authority.

The opposing party, the Federalists, believed the Constitution was clear. Any powers not given to the federal government belonged to the states. In other words, state residents maintained a great deal of control over their own laws and customs.

When the argument persisted, James Madison suggested changes to the Constitution's wording. But, even though Madison had written much of the original Constitution, his changes needed Congressional approval. Madison therefore turned his suggestions into a list of proposed **amendments**. Ten of these were accepted by Congress and **ratified** by the states and became known as the Bill of Rights. The First Amendment guaranteed citizens freedom of religion: "Congress shall make no law respecting an establishment of religion, or prohibiting the free exercise thereof. . ."

James Madison wrote most of the US Constitution as well as the 10 amendments known as the Bill of Rights.

ROOTS OF RELIGIOUS FREEDOM

American colonists were unique in their motivation for leaving their places of birth. They were not trying to spread the customs of their homeland. In fact, they were willing to cross 3,000 miles of ocean to leave these political and religious views behind.

The great majority of our original settlers were English. In the centuries leading up to the Revolutionary War, Great Britain had one recognized church: the Church of England.

At the first Thanksgiving in the new colony in 1621, Pilgrims and Native Americans gathered to share a meal.

HENRY VIII AND THE CHURCH OF ENGLAND

England had once been predominantly Catholic. In the 1530s, however, King Henry VIII needed a male heir. For that to happen, he also needed a new wife. Henry sought a divorce, but the pope, the leader of the Catholic faith, refused to grant it.

Henry's solution was simple: he would create his own Church of England. It would be a Protestant church, meaning the pope had no authority over it. The church would be headed by Henry himself.

Fast Fact

ANNE BOLEYN

Anne Boleyn, for whom King Henry VIII broke England away from the Catholic church, never bore Henry a son. Instead, she gave birth to the future Queen Elizabeth I, who would reign for 44 years. Anne and Henry were married for nearly three years when Henry had the marriage annulled. Anne was beheaded on May 19, 1536.

The full name of Henry VIII was Henry Tudor. Born on June 28, 1491, he was the son of Henry VII and Elizabeth York. He had six siblings, but only three survived. His older brother, Arthur, was supposed to become king, but he died when he was 15 years old, and Henry took over the reign at the age of 10.

Although Henry's reasons were personal, the resulting partnership between church and monarchy affected everyone. With such a great concentration of power, Henry could do anything he liked, whether or not it benefited his subjects. It was the abuse of this power by Henry and subsequent monarchs that prompted thousands of **emigrants** to seek a new life in the colonies.

Henry VIII is remembered by many as the king whose stubborn and persistent pursuit of a male heir led him to have six wives. He was much more than that. While not his main intention, Henry's break with the pope opened the floodgates to a variety of Protestant groups. That, in turn, led to more diversity of belief, and ultimately, to greater religious freedom.

RELIGION AND THE FIRST AMENDMENT

After winning independence from Great Britain, our Founding Fathers were determined not to repeat the mistakes of their native country. This meant creating a clear division between government and religion—a concept also known as the separation of church and state.

The First Amendment offers the citizens of the United States two very specific guarantees regarding freedom of religion. These are known as the "Establishment Clause" and the "Free Exercise Clause."

ESTABLISHMENT CLAUSE

The Establishment Clause prevents the United States Congress from:

- Creating a national religion
- Demanding that people follow—or financially support—one specific faith
- Collecting taxes to support a church

The Establishment Clause also provides that citizens cannot be barred from voting or holding elected office because of their religious views, or prevented from owning a home or holding a job because of their religion.

The Founding Fathers appeared on the $2 bill.

FREE EXERCISE CLAUSE

The Free Exercise Clause allows citizens to demonstrate their faith as they see fit. There are restrictions, however. Clear-cut evidence of danger, illegal activity, or an unfair burden on others can outweigh the free expression of religion.

Fast Fact

THE CLAUSES AND THE COURTS

The Establishment Clause seems self-evident, yet between 1925 and 2014, more than 50 cases debating this right reached the Supreme Court (shown here). Between 1878 and 2012, the Supreme Court decided nearly 40 cases involving the Free Exercise Clause.

CHAPTER 2
STRUGGLES WITH RELIGIOUS FREEDOM

THE PURITANS

The Puritans were English Protestants who believed King Henry VIII's Church of England retained too many Catholic customs. When their attempts to reform the church failed, thousands sailed to America in the 1630s. Remarkably, although the Puritans came to Massachusetts Bay Colony to practice their own beliefs freely, they had little tolerance for the faiths of others.

ROGER WILLIAMS

When Roger Williams arrived in Massachusetts in 1631, he was outraged by the punishments his fellow Puritans inflicted on Quakers and Baptists, whom they denounced as heretics. He was also vocal about what he saw as a lack of separation between the Puritan church and the colony's governance. In 1635, he was banished from Massachusetts Bay Colony.

Roger Williams (right) is sheltered by Native Americans in 1636 after fleeing the Massachusetts Bay Colony to avoid arrest.

NEW SETTLEMENT

The following spring, in 1636, Williams established his own settlement that he named Providence, in what is now Rhode Island. In Williams's colony, laws were established by majority vote. Residents were also guaranteed "liberty of conscience," meaning they were free to form their own religious and political beliefs. It was the first town in America to offer a complete separation between the roles of church and state. Roger Williams's philosophies in great part influenced the enactment of the First Amendment.

The statue of Roger Williams overlooks Prospect Terrace Park in present-day Providence, Rhode Island.

Fast Fact

MARY DYER

The Puritans held a particular animosity for Baptists and Quakers, whom they routinely whipped, mutilated, and jailed. On June 1, 1660, Puritan-turned-Quaker Mary Dyer was publicly hanged in Boston for defying a ban on her religion. Just before she died, Dyer asked God to forgive those who took her life.

WILLIAM PENN'S HOLY EXPERIMENT

Unlike the Puritans, William Penn envisioned the colonies as a safe haven for members of all religions. Much to his father's dismay, Penn became a Quaker at the age of 22. In England, this was cause for imprisonment. Penn spent nearly a year in jail for refusing to deny his beliefs.

In 1681, Penn received a land grant consisting of over 45,000 square miles from King Charles II to repay a debt owed to Penn's father. The king named the new colony Pennsylvania. Penn called it his "Holy Experiment." He invited persecuted peoples from around the world and guaranteed them freedom of religion, fair jury trials, and free elections, among other rights. He also created a framework of government that included the concept of amendments. These, Penn believed, would allow laws to develop peacefully as society itself evolved. Penn's concept of amendments would be borrowed by James Madison and Congress when it came time to create the Bill of Rights.

Penn's statue (shown here) sits on top of the Philadelphia City Hall.

PENN'S MESSAGE REACHES GERMANY

Many religions believe that infants should be baptized as soon as possible after birth. Anabaptists believe that baptism should be delayed until a person is old enough to profess his or her faith. This seemingly harmless difference of opinion outraged Roman Catholics, Lutherans, and others. They tortured and executed Anabaptists by the thousands. Some were drowned. Others were burned alive.

Many Anabaptists fled to German-speaking regions. It was there that they heard about a man named William Penn who offered religious freedom in his new colony. The first Anabaptist immigrants arrived in 1683. Ancestors of the Amish, Mennonite, and Brethren groups still live in Pennsylvania today.

Many Anabaptists were tortured and executed, often by burning at the stake, as shown in this 1685 painting.

BAPTISTS AND SLAVERY

Today, the United States is one of the most religiously diverse nations in the world. That doesn't mean, however, that religious conflicts are nonexistent. Leading up to the Civil War, the Baptist Church split over the issue of slavery. Baptists in the North felt that God would not condone the buying and selling of human beings. Southern Baptists, however, relied upon slave labor and saw no biblical conflict. The Southern Baptist Convention was formed in 1845 by pro-slavery **congregants**. It was not until 1995 that Southern Baptists formally renounced the denial of civil rights to African Americans.

MODERN-DAY TERRORISM

More recently, the terrorist attacks of September 11, 2001, killed nearly 3,000 people in New York City and Washington, DC. Since then, hundreds more have died in attacks in the United States in Boston, San Bernadino, and Orlando, as well as others in European cities such as London, Madrid, Paris, and Brussels. These acts of violence have created, for many citizens, a distrust of Muslims. During the 2016 presidential campaign, candidate Donald Trump even called for a "total and complete shutdown of Muslims entering the United States until our country's representatives can figure out what is going on."

On June 12, 2016, a lone gunman killed 49 people and wounded 53 at Pulse, a gay nightclub in Orlando, Florida.

REFUGEES

In 2011, civil war broke out in the Middle Eastern country of Syria, and nearly half of its population was displaced. Refugees fleeing the violence sought asylum in neighboring countries, but many in the United States worried about accepting Syrian refugees because of concerns of possible terrorism. The First Amendment guarantees religious freedom, but it cannot eliminate fear of practices we do not understand. It can, however, provide a legal means to address perceived prejudicial treatment.

In 2005, five Ohio inmates sued for the right to exercise their religions freely. What made the case interesting was the unusual nature of the prisoners' religions: one was a Satanist, two followed a Viking religion worshipping the mythological god Thor, another was a Wiccan witch, and the fifth belonged to a white separatist church. The Supreme Court unanimously ruled that the First Amendment protected the prisoners' right to exercise their religions, even if they were not mainstream.

The Supreme Court ruled that Ohio inmates' religious freedom was protected under the First Amendment.

THE RIGHT TO NOT BELIEVE

Freedom *of* religion also means freedom *from* religion. The Establishment Clause of the First Amendment makes it clear that no one can be forced to practice any specific faith, or even to believe in God at all. Those who don't believe in God are called atheists. Those who feel there is no proof of the existence of God are called agnostics. Two important Supreme Court cases have established atheists' and agnostics' right to exclude themselves from religious observance.

Fast Fact

TORCASA V. WATKINS

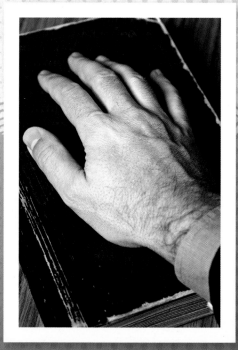

For years, it was Maryland's practice to require that anyone holding public office publicly affirm their belief in God. When Roy Torcasa was appointed **notary public**, it was demanded that he make this pledge. Torcasa, an atheist, refused. His appointment as notary was revoked. After several Maryland courts ruled against Torcasa, he filed an appeal with the United States Supreme Court in April 1961. The justices unanimously ruled that by requiring officeholders to profess a belief in God, Maryland was violating the Establishment Clause of the First Amendment.

WALLACE V. JAFFREE

In 1985, the Supreme Court took up the case of Ishmael Jaffree. Jaffree was a resident of Mobile County, Alabama, and the father of three children. Each morning, Alabama schools started the day with a minute of meditation. In some classrooms, including those of his children, teachers led prayers during this time. Jaffree was an agnostic. He sued the school, claiming that his children were being forced to participate in religious activities. The Supreme Court agreed with Jaffree. They found that by requiring prayer, Alabama schools were endorsing religion and violating the First Amendment.

The US Supreme Court ruled that Alabama schools could not force students to participate in prayers in the classroom.

CHAPTER 3
RELIGION AND GOVERNMENT

Look at the back of the dollar bill in your pocket and you will see that it includes the motto "In God We Trust." You might ask how this is possible if there is a separation between church and state. This was the same question asked by Stefan Ray Aronow in 1970. He was the first to file a lawsuit claiming that the motto violated the Establishment Clause.

The California District Court found that, regardless of Aronow's claims, he had no legal standing to file the case. Although Aronow was a US citizen and taxpayer, the motto's appearance on currency and coins was dictated by federal law. Aronow, an individual, lacked the power or authority to overturn this law.

The phrase "In God We Trust" is the official motto of the United States. It appears on US coins and paper currency, such as the back of the $1 bill. It was first used on coins in 1864 and on paper money in 1957.

During the 1950s, many Americans worried that communists were infiltrating American culture and society. To demonstrate the difference between the atheistic Soviet Union and the United States, President Dwight D. Eisenhower signed a law in 1956, making "In God We Trust" the national motto. The motto was reaffirmed by the US Senate 50 years later.

Aronow **appealed** the decision. The appeals court judged the case on its **merits**, not on Aronow's ability to file the lawsuit. The judges found that the use of the motto on currency and coins "has nothing whatsoever to do with the establishment of religion. Its use is of a patriotic or ceremonial character and bears no true resemblance to a governmental sponsorship of a religious exercise." Like the Declaration of Independence, the motto mentions God. Yet, while the motto may be inspirational, the Court concluded that "In God We Trust" has no religious impact on those who view it.

LEGISLATIVE PRAYER

On May 1, 1789, Reverend William Linn was appointed Chaplain of the US House of Representatives. Since then, the House has been served by chaplains from at least 11 **denominations**. These chaplains open each session with prayer. They also offer counsel and oversee memorial services when a member of the House (or an employee) dies. The Senate also has a chaplain. Is this is a violation of the separation of church and state?

Chaplains of the House of Representatives often lead the members in prayer, as pictured here in 1919.

ANOTHER CHALLENGE

In 1983, Ernest Chambers was a member of the Nebraska legislature. He believed that the state-paid chaplain and the daily opening prayer violated the Establishment Clause. The case reached the Supreme Court, which disagreed with Chambers's position.

Chief Justice Warren Burger based the Court's **opinion** on historical custom. Burger noted that a chaplain had been hired by the First Continental Congress. This, he said, proved that our Founding Fathers viewed legislative prayer as "no real threat to the Establishment Clause." Based on this reasoning, Chambers lost his appeal.

RELIGIOUS DISPLAYS

The presence of religious symbols in public buildings such as courthouses is regularly challenged. Display of the Ten Commandments is particularly contentious. Two 2005 Supreme Court cases prove that this issue is far from simple.

In 1961, a six-foot-tall stone slab containing the Ten Commandments was donated to the state of Texas. The gift was in part funded by movie director Cecil B. DeMille, who made the famous film *The Ten Commandments*. In addition to the text of the commandments, the monument also contained a Star of David, an eagle holding the American flag, and other symbols.

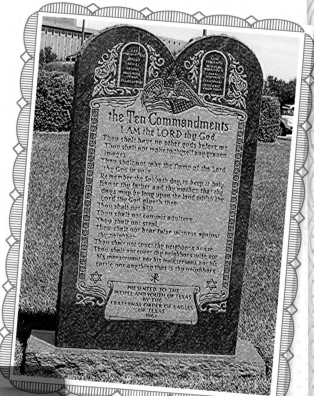

This monument of the Ten Commandments was donated to the state of Texas and placed in front of the State Capitol in Austin, Texas.

PROVOCATIVE MONUMENT

Thomas Van Orden frequently walked past the monument on his way to the Texas Supreme Court's law library. He believed the placement of the Ten Commandments on State Capitol grounds indicated that the government endorsed religion. The district court, and the appeals court after that, ruled against Van Orden.

The case made its way to the US Supreme Court, which also ruled against Van Orden. The Court based its decision on the monument's historic value. Additionally, the justices decided that religious text on a monument does not necessarily violate the Establishment Clause.

KENTUCKY CHALLENGE

At the same time, another important case was being **litigated**. The American Civil Liberties Union filed suit against three Kentucky counties displaying the Ten Commandments in courthouses and publicly funded schools (*McCreary County v. ACLU of Kentucky*). This time, the Supreme Court found the practice to be a violation of the First Amendment. It was a 5-4 split decision, but the court found the display unconstitutional. By displaying the Ten Commandments, the Court ruled, Kentucky's state government could be assumed to be endorsing religion.

NOT-SO-HAPPY HOLIDAYS

Even more than the Ten Commandments, holiday displays generate a great number of First Amendment challenges. Is it proper to erect Christmas trees, menorahs, and nativity scenes on public land and buildings? How could customs so happy and festive create such controversy?

The first case involving Christmas decorations reached the Supreme Court in 1984. For 40 years, the city of Pawtucket, Rhode Island, erected a Christmas display. Located in the shopping district, the display included Santa's house, a "Seasons Greetings" sign, and a nativity scene. Daniel Donnelly, who had lived in Pawtucket for only four years, took offense at the display. He believed it violated the Establishment Clause of the First Amendment.

Festive displays similar to this one offend some people.

COURT RULES DISPLAYS NONRELIGIOUS

The first two courts that heard the case agreed with Donnelly and ordered the city to remove the nativity. The Supreme Court took a different view. The display was obviously aimed at Christmas shoppers, the Court said. As such, Pawtucket was not trying to impose a state religion on its residents. Instead, the Court felt the display served a secular—nonreligious—function. The Supreme Court overturned the decisions of the lower courts.

INCLUDING OTHER RELIGIOUS GROUPS

A later, more complicated, case resulted in seemingly contradictory decisions. In 1989, Allegheny County in Pennsylvania exhibited not one but two holiday displays on the grounds of public buildings. There was a nativity scene inside the county courthouse and a large menorah and Christmas tree outside the City-County building. The American Civil Liberties Union (ACLU) felt the county government was endorsing religion. The Supreme Court found that the display of the nativity scene inside the courthouse did violate the Establishment Clause. But the menorah, because it was placed beside a Christmas tree, was a secular display and could remain in place.

A menorah is used during the Jewish holiday of Hanukkah.

WHY DON'T CHURCHES PAY TAXES?

Why are religious organizations exempt from income and other taxes? This is a question that many citizens ponder. After all, if the federal government cannot establish or endorse a religion, how can one of its agencies give churches special treatment?

The reasoning behind their tax-exempt status is that the exemption keeps the government out of the financial affairs of churches, thereby ensuring the separation of church and state. Others argue the opposite: that tax exemptions violate the separation of church and state because the exemptions are a privilege, not a right.

Taxes are collected by a federal agency called the Internal Revenue Service (IRS). It is the IRS that grants tax exemptions to places of worship, members of the clergy, and religious organizations. These special tax laws recognize the unique protections offered by the First Amendment.

Nativity scenes such as this are not considered secular displays.

CONDITIONS FOR TAX EXEMPTION

In order to remain tax-exempt, certain conditions must be met; otherwise, the IRS can revoke the tax exemption:

- The main mission of the organization must be religious or charitable.
- Earnings cannot substantially benefit one individual.
- The organization's primary function cannot be to influence creation of laws (known as "lobbying").
- The organization cannot participate in political campaigns or support or denounce any particular candidate.
- The organization's activities must be legal and in keeping with established public policy.

BOB JONES UNIVERSITY V. UNITED STATES

Bob Jones University did not allow African American students to attend. So, in 1970, the IRS revoked its tax exemption because it discriminated on the basis of race. Bob Jones University, the IRS declared, would now pay taxes. Bob Jones University filed a lawsuit, claiming the decision infringed on the school's right to exercise its religious beliefs freely.

Bob Jones University was founded by Bob Jones Sr. in 1926. The university is a private Protestant college in Greenville, South Carolina.

AFTERMATH

When the case reached the Supreme Court, the justices stated that religious schools have a particular obligation to end racial discrimination. It was the Court's opinion that the IRS was right in revoking the university's tax-exempt status.

The school relented, and in 1971, it allowed African American students to attend. However, it still banned interracial dating. That ban remained in effect until 2000, when presidential candidate George W. Bush visited the campus. The resulting public uproar spurred university administrators to change that policy.

Fast Fact

CONTROVERSIAL CHURCH

Scientology was founded in 1952 by science fiction writer L. Ron Hubbard. It was controversial from the start and has had many run-ins with the law over the years. Scientology gained huge publicity after it targeted Hollywood celebrities such as Tom Cruise and John Travolta. It was recognized as a religion by the IRS in 1993, but several other countries do not recognize it. It has branches all over the world, including its headquarters in Hollywood (shown here).

CHAPTER 4

RELIGION AND THE WORKPLACE

CIVIL RIGHTS ACT OF 1964

The First Amendment is not the only law protecting religious liberties. During John F. Kennedy's 1960 presidential campaign, he promised equality to all. Once in office, he proposed a **civil rights** act. Before it could become law, however, Kennedy was assassinated. His successor, Lyndon B. Johnson, successfully passed the Civil Rights Act of 1964, which guaranteed all Americans religious rights.

JFK AND CIVIL RIGHTS

Kennedy adopted vigorous action to guarantee civil rights for all. He wanted to restore the nation back to what he felt was its original mission as laid out in the Declaration of Independence and the Constitution: defending and upholding human rights. Theories and conspiracies abound for the reason behind his murder, but it is possible his stance on civil rights may have been a factor.

President Kennedy is shown here addressing the nation about civil rights on June 11, 1963.

JFK AND CATHOLICISM

When John F. Kennedy was elected president in November 1960, he became the first (and still only) Roman Catholic to gain that office. His religion played a large role in the election campaign.

JFK repeatedly endorsed the separation of church and state and argued that the oath of office to uphold the Constitution took precedence over his religious beliefs. During the campaign, he repeatedly had to reassure voters that he would not be taking orders from the Pope. His candidacy was opposed by one of the leading Protestant leaders, Norman Vincent Peale, on the grounds of his religion.

JFK's experiences, as well as his interaction with Martin Luther King Jr. and other African American civil rights leaders, made him more than eager to get the Civil Rights Act passed.

During his presidency, Kennedy regularly attended mass at St. Matthew's Cathedral in Washington, DC. His funeral services were also held there.

PROTECTED RELIGIOUS PRACTICES AT WORK

The Civil Rights Act prohibits discrimination against employees based on their religion. All religions are protected, whether established, new, or outside the mainstream. Only an employee's sincere religious belief is required for protection under the Civil Rights Act.

People's religious beliefs are often reflected in their appearance. Sikh men traditionally wear a turban, Rastafarians sport dreadlocks, and many Jewish men wear yarmulkes. Some Christians wear religious jewelry such as crosses and crucifixes. Employers and employees cannot discriminate against others for practicing their faith. All employees must be treated equally.

A Muslim woman cannot be fired because people are uncomfortable with her hijab (head covering).

EMPLOYMENT DIVISION V. SMITH

In the Native American Church, peyote—a drug that produces hallucinations—is used in certain rituals. In the 1980s, two employees of a private drug rehabilitation clinic in Oregon ingested peyote. Both were Native Americans, and both were fired.

The employees, Galen Black and Alfred Smith, sued the clinic, claiming their right to to freely exercise their faith was infringed. Their case reached the Supreme Court in 1989. In a 6–3 decision, the Court found that one's religious beliefs do not outweigh existing law. If exceptions were made to every regulation based on religious practice, nearly all laws could be challenged. The Court said that civic duties such as payment of taxes or abiding by child labor laws could not be ignored. In this instance, the best interests of society superseded the religious freedoms given to employees.

Peyote is a cactus that grows in Texas and Mexico. It contains a drug that can cause hallucinations. It is often used in certain Native American rituals.

CHAPTER 5

RELIGION AND SCHOOLS

A large number of First Amendment challenges involve schools. An early case illustrates America's long battle to balance education and religion.

THE BIBLE WARS

In the 1840s, residents of Philadelphia found themselves in the midst of a violent battle between Catholics and Protestants. A wave of about 2 million Irish Catholic immigrants arrived in American cities and sparked a backlash of strong anti-Catholic sentiment. At the time, schools started each day by reading a passage from the Protestant Bible. A Roman Catholic bishop, Francis Kenrick, wrote to school officials asking that Catholic children be able to read from their own Bible.

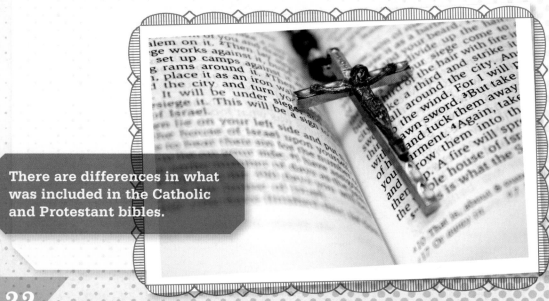

There are differences in what was included in the Catholic and Protestant bibles.

INCREASED CONFLICT

In 1844, Hugh Clark, a school director for a Catholic school in the neighborhood of Kensington, suggested that all reading of the Bible be temporarily halted until a compromise acceptable to both religions be reached.

Protestants had already spread rumors that the Catholics wanted to remove the Bible from schools. They used Clark's suggestion to further incite civil unrest. But things took an ugly turn when riots—known as "Bible Wars"—broke out. Catholic homes and churches were burned. Rioting continued for two months. Dozens of men were killed or wounded. Property was destroyed. The Pennsylvania state militia eventually restored peace, but many Philadelphia citizens were shocked that the Bible, of all things, could instigate such violence.

On May 7, 1844, Protestant mobs burned two Catholic churches in Philadelphia. On July 7, 1844, rioting broke out again, and the state militia was called in to intervene.

THE PLEDGE OF ALLEGIANCE

The controversy over the Pledge of Allegiance is perhaps even better known than that over the Bible. Although the pledge was written in the 1890s, Congress did not make it our official pledge until 1942. Originally, the pledge was as follows: "I pledge allegiance to the flag of the United States of America and to the Republic for which it stands, one Nation, indivisible, with liberty and justice for all."

During our **Cold War** with the Soviet Union, the words "under God" were added to the pledge. Unlike the communists, who promoted atheism, Congress wanted to illustrate that America believed in a Creator.

Students pledge allegiance to the flag in 1899 in Washington, DC. The original pledge was written by Francis Bellamy in 1892.

MICHAEL NEWDOW

In 2000, Michael Newdow (an atheist) sued his daughter's school over its morning recital of the pledge. Because it includes the words "under God," Newdow believed the school violated the First Amendment's Establishment Clause. The Supreme Court found that Newdow had no legal standing to bring such a lawsuit. Several justices did write opinions, however, stating that it is constitutional for schools to require teachers to lead students in the pledge.

Michael Newdow speaks at the Atheist Alliance International Convention in Long Beach, California.

Fast Fact

ATHEISM

Atheists do not believe that God and other deities exist based on evidence. This does not mean, however, that all atheists are anti-religion. In fact, atheists are found among the clergy. Today, there are still countries where atheists can be put to death because of their beliefs.

PRAYER IN SCHOOL

The First Amendment protects everyone's right to a peaceful expression of religious beliefs—even if those beliefs offend others. So how does this apply to prayer in schools?

In 1962, New York schools started each day with a non-denominational prayer. It said, "Almighty God, we acknowledge our dependence upon Thee, and beg Thy blessings upon us, our teachers, and our country." Students who felt uncomfortable reciting the prayer were allowed to excuse themselves. Even with this exception, however, several parents found the practice objectionable. They believed the school was violating the First Amendment's Establishment Clause.

School opened with prayer at this private school in Pie Town, New Mexico, in June 1940.

PRAYER DEBATES

The New York appeals court disagreed with the parents. They did not believe the morning prayer was unconstitutional. When the case eventually reached the Supreme Court, the justices interpreted it differently. They found that allowing students to excuse themselves did not make the school's actions constitutional. By writing the prayer and asking students to recite it, the school was indeed endorsing a specific belief system. This contradicts the First Amendment's protection against the government establishing a religion.

A 1962 case, known as *Engel v. Vitale*, was a landmark decision, making it unlawful for schools to compose prayers to be recited by students. But it did not—as many claim—eliminate prayer from schools. It is still lawful for students to pray, individually or in groups, as long as they do so peacefully and without disrupting others.

The 1962 Supreme Court ruling made it illegal for school officials to write prayers to be used in schools.

SCHOOL VOUCHERS

The subject of school vouchers is hotly debated. Vouchers are provided by a school district to cover tuition at private schools of a parent's choosing. These vouchers are distributed based on financial need.

In 2002, taxpayers questioned the constitutionality of Ohio's school voucher program. Since 96 percent of the families receiving vouchers chose religious-based schools, these taxpayers felt that the state was endorsing religion—a clear violation of the First Amendment. *Zelman v. Simmons-Harris* was a case that involved school vouchers.

The school voucher plan provides money for students to attend schools of their choice.

William Rehnquist was the chief justice presiding over the *Zelman v. Simmons-Harris* case. He is shown here administering the oath of office to Vice President Al Gore on January 20, 1993.

In a close decision in *Zelman v. Simmons-Harris*, the Supreme Court found Ohio's voucher program to be constitutional. Since parents could choose any institution, religious or not, it was the families who were endorsing church-run schools, not the state of Ohio.

That ruling was in 2002, and while this seems to be the final decision on school vouchers, it is likely more cases will make their way to the Supreme Court. As the justices change, so, too, may the interpretation of the law.

CHAPTER 6
RELIGION AND DAILY LIFE

Americans practice a large diversity of religious faiths. About three-quarters of the US population is Christian, divided between Protestants (about one-half) and Catholics (around one-quarter). The largest other Christian groups are Mormons, Jehovah's Witnesses, and Orthodox, but many other religious **sects** exist. Non-Christian faiths represent only a tiny percentage of the total population, the largest being Jewish (1.7 percent), Muslim (0.6 percent), Buddhist (0.7 percent), and Hindu (0.4 percent). There are also nondenominational believers and those who do not believe in God at all.

This pie chart represents religious affiliations in the United States in 2014, but other sources may have slightly different numbers.

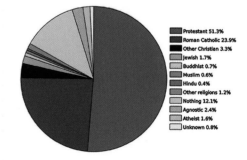

Protestant 51.3%
Roman Catholic 23.9%
Other Christian 3.3%
Jewish 1.7%
Buddhist 0.7%
Muslim 0.6%
Hindu 0.4%
Other religions 1.2%
Nothing 12.1%
Agnostic 2.4%
Atheist 1.6%
Unknown 0.8%

We have come a long way since the 1600s, when the Puritans first stepped onto the shores of New England and forced everyone to attend the same Sunday service. Those early colonists likely never imagined that the Constitution would guarantee freedom of religion to all while completely separating church and state.

RESTRICTIONS ON RELIGIOUS EXERCISE

While the United States is a successful melting pot of ethnicities and religious faiths, not all religious practices are protected by the First Amendment. Illegal activities, or those causing harm or hardship, are restricted. A case in point is **polygamy**, the practice of marrying more than one person at the same time, which is against the law in America. Yet Mormon men once believed it was their religious duty to take several wives.

In 1874, Mormon George Reynolds was **indicted** by the state of Utah for breaking its bigamy laws. His case eventually made its way to the US Supreme Court (*Reynolds v. United States*). The justices found that Reynold's religious duty did not supersede the nation's long-accepted laws limiting a person to one spouse. To make such an exception for Mormons would, they said, open the floodgates to other unwanted or even dangerous behaviors that could include human sacrifice or murder. Religious beliefs cannot be superior to the law itself.

The Mormon Temple was built in Salt Lake City, Utah, in the nineteenth century. It was officially dedicated in April 1893.

LIMITS AND OBLIGATIONS

There are other limits on the free exercise of religion. For instance, the government has no obligation to preserve public land for religious rituals. Traditional laws dating back into English history required a day of rest on the Christian Sabbath, Sunday. This led to a whole host of Sunday closing laws and other restrictions.

In *McGowan v. Maryland* (1961), the US Supreme Court acknowledged the historical religious motivation behind those laws, but ruled that most modern Sunday closing laws were secular in nature. Then, in 1985, the Court ruled (in *Estate of Thornton v. Caldor, Inc.*) that a Connecticut law that gave employees the right not to work on their chosen Sabbath was unconstitutional because it put religious concerns ahead of secular ones.

Restrictions on Sunday openings were originally designed to honor the Christian Sabbath and promote church attendance.

LIMITED RESTRICTIONS

Prayer in schools is allowed if it is practiced without bothering or annoying others, but student religious organizations may not discriminate based on lifestyle or beliefs. This was decided in a 2010 case called *Christian Legal Society v. Martinez*.

The Christian Legal Society is a nondenominational group of law professors, students, lawyers, and judges who promote Christian values in the legal profession. When the CLS created a chapter at University of California, Hastings College of Law in San Francisco, California, it required that members abide by specific rules of conduct. Because this code of conduct prohibited gay students from becoming voting members, Hastings refused to recognize the CLS as a student organization.

In 2008, CLS sued the college, claiming that Hastings was violating not only its freedom of religion, but also its freedoms of speech and assembly. The case eventually reached the Supreme Court, which was not swayed by CLS's arguments. Justice John Paul Stevens reasoned that if the CLS code of conduct could be used to ban gay students, it could also potentially be used to exclude African Americans, women, or anyone else the group deemed unfit. In a 5–4 decision, the Court ruled that the college was correct in demanding that student organizations be neutral and accept all comers.

CHAPTER 7

CONCLUSION

RELIGIOUS WARS

Some scholars believe that as many as 11 million people were killed during Europe's Thirty Years' War between Roman Catholics and Protestants (1618–1648). During the Crusades in the 1000s and 1200s, nearly 200 years of war between Christians and Muslims resulted in some 3 million deaths. More recently, the Lebanese Civil War (1975–1990) between Sunni Muslims, Shiites, Jews, Christians, and Druze took nearly a quarter of a million lives.

History has proven that when the powers of church and state cross, violence and religious intolerance often result. This lesson was not lost on our Founding Fathers. America has escaped "holy wars" in great part because of the foresight of the Founders in enacting the First Amendment.

The First Crusade led to the recapture of Jerusalem by the Crusaders in 1099.

GEORGE WASHINGTON'S PLEDGE

In 1789 and 1790, as part of the campaign to ratify the Bill of Rights, George Washington wrote to every major religious organization in the country. To the Baptists, Presbyterians, Quakers, Roman Catholics, Jews, and other religious leaders, he made this promise: "Everyone shall sit in safety under his own vine and fig tree and there shall be none to make him afraid." Washington was quoting Old Testament prophet Micah (4:4), indicating a desire for peace and security.

George Washington wrote the "vine and fig tree" letter shortly after being elected the first president of the United States in 1789.

The First Amendment may be interpreted differently by future Supreme Court justices. Our society may continue to diversify. Our norms may continue to evolve. But Washington's message serves as a timeless reminder of our Constitutional right to freedom of religion, and America's unique place in world history.

The United States of America has long been recognized as one of the most religiously diverse societies in the world thanks in no small part to the First Amendment guarantees.

GLOSSARY

amendment—a change or addition to the US Constitution

appeal—request for review by a higher court

civil rights—rights to personal liberty and equality

Cold War—hostile rivalry between nations, but without war

congregant—one who worships with others of the same religion

denomination—a religious group, usually with more than one church

emigrant—a person who leaves his or her native country

indict—to formally charge with a crime or wrongdoing

litigate—to carry out a lawsuit

merits—the fundamental issues of a legal case

notary public—a public official authorized to authenticate documents

opinion—a written explanation of a court's decision

polygamy—marriage in which a person has more than one spouse at the same time

ratify—to confirm or approve

sect—a small, nontraditional religious group

FURTHER INFORMATION

Books

Berkin, Carol. *The Bill of Rights; The Fight to Secure America's Liberties*. New York: Simon & Schuster, 2015.

Dooling, Sandra. *James Madison*. New York: Rosen Publishing, 2013.

Keegan, Anna. *The United States Constitution and the Bill of Rights*. New York: Rosen Publishing, 2016.

Krull, Kathleen. *A Kids' Guide to America's Bill of Rights.* New York: HarperCollins, 2015.

Online

Anglican Church in Virginia
www.history.org/almanack/life/religion/religiondfn.cfm/

Bill of Rights Institute
www.billofrightsinstitute.org/founding-documents/bill-of-rights/

Britannica.com, "Bill of Rights"
www.britannica.com/topic/Bill-of-Rights-United-States-Constitution

Cornell University Law School, Legal Information Institute
www.law.cornell.edu/constitution/billofrights

History.com, "Bill of Rights"
www.history.com/topics/bill-of-rights

Library of Congress, "Bill of Rights"
www.loc.gov/exhibits/creating-the-united-states/creating-the-bill-of-rights.html

National Archives and Records Administration
www.archives.gov/exhibits/charters/bill_of_rights_transcript.html

INDEX